Mysterious Spinners

For three cuties, Evan, Margaret and Miranda . . . and with thanks to Anne Osborne, Ph.D.,

a specialist in Chinese history and professor of Asian and World History

at Rider University, for sharing her expertise—W.P.

To Peter, who made sure I had something to eat and something to laugh about—J.K.

For information contact:
MONDO Publishing
980 Avenue of the Americas
New York, NY 10018

Visit our website at www.mondopub.com

Printed in China

07 08 09 10 11 12 HC 9 8 7 6 5 4 3 2 1
09 10 11 12 PB 9 8 7 6 5 4 3 2

ISBN 1-59336-315-X (HC)   1-59336-316-8 (PB)

Designed by Annette Cyr

Library of Congress Cataloging-in-Publication Data

Pfeffer, Wendy, 1929-
    Mysterious spinners / by Wendy Pfeffer ; illustrated by Julie Kim.
        p. cm.
    Summary: Relates the legend of how silk was discovered by a young empress in ancient
China. Also includes facts about silk and the life cycle of the silkworm.
    ISBN 1-59336-315-X -- ISBN 1-59336-316-8 (pbk.)
        [1. Folklore--China. 2. Silk--Folklore. 3. Kings, queens, rulers, etc.--Folklore. 4.
Silkworms.] I. Kim, Julie J., 1973- ill. II. Title.

PZ8.1.P545My 2005
398.2'0951'092--dc22

2003071019

Mysterious Spinners

A Chinese Legend Retold by Wendy Pfeffer

Illustrated by Julie Kim

NEW YORK

Thousands of years ago, China's beautiful legendary empress, Hsi-ling Shih, sat with her ladies-in-waiting, sipping tea under the wide-spreading branches of a mulberry tree. The mulberry leaves rippled lightly in the spring breeze.

Hsi-ling was enjoying the warm sun when suddenly something shiny caught her eye. A ray of sunlight illuminated a small creature on one of the tree's lower branches. And what a strange sight it was! One long strand of shiny thread oozed from a white worm's lower lip.

Hsi-ling watched in wonder as the worm wrapped the thread around and around itself. She looked further and realized that the whole tree was covered with white worms wrapping themselves in long, shiny threads.

All day the curious empress watched the amazing sight. When evening fell she returned to the palace. Haunted by the mysterious scene, Hsi-ling found that sleep came slowly that night. She wondered if the tiny worms would be winding and wrapping when sunlight filled the morning sky.

When the sun's first rays appeared in the east, Hsi-ling hurried her ladies outside. The fascinating creatures were still winding and wrapping. For three days Hsi-ling watched the worms at work. For three nights she dreamed about the mysterious little spinners.

On the fourth day Hsi-ling searched every tree. Her ladies looked high and low, but the worms were nowhere in sight. In their place creamy white cocoons, shimmering in the sunlight, hung on every branch. Hsi-ling dashed to the tree and fetched a cocoon. She turned it over and over in her hands. She ran her fingertips around it and was amazed to feel circles of thin, sticky thread.

Then she did something unexpected. Hsi-ling dropped the cocoon in her tea. Why she did this no one knows. Maybe it was an accident. Perhaps she only wanted to wash off the stickiness. Possibly a sudden insight came over the curious Hsi-ling that made her do something so strange. Whatever the reason, once in the hot tea, the smooth thread began to unravel.

Determined to find out what was happening, Hsi-ling poked a twig into the tea and caught the end of the thread. She unwound one lovely, long thread. It was as light as air, as soft as a breeze. She pulled and pulled until it covered her gown and her tiny feet. She was amazed. In all her life she had never seen such a sight. That one thread was long enough to fly a kite high up in the sky.

She called her ladies-in-waiting to gaze at its beauty. Hsi-ling gathered the thread in her hands and held its delicate softness close to her cheek. Then she tugged at the thread. She couldn't break it. Hsi-ling decided it was strong enough to be woven on a loom.

She envisioned a splendid gift woven with this fine thread for her husband, Huang Ti, the legendary emperor of China. And she knew just how she would make it. She told her ladies her plan. Delighted, they danced in a circle.

Determined to go ahead with the plan, Hsi-ling and her ladies began plucking all the cocoons in sight. Their arms were piled high as they carried them into the palace. Flowers, in every color of the rainbow, lined the curving path. They bobbed and bowed as the ladies hurried by.

Inside the palace Hsi-ling directed her ladies to boil water and drop the cocoons in. The white bundles bobbled around in the pot. Then the ladies dipped sticks in the water, found the thread ends, and unwound the threads, just as Hsi-ling had done.

Hsi-ling instructed her ladies to unwind the bundle coverings five at a time. Then, as one lady held Hsi-ling's golden ring and fed the five threads through its loop, another lady twisted the delicate threads until they were blended into one. The last lady twirled a mulberry twig, causing the five-thread strand to be wound onto it.

For days Hsi-ling and her ladies surrounded themselves with the creamy white bundles. But even a thousand of these cocoons did not make enough thread for the royal gift. Hsi-ling and her ladies searched the palace gardens for more bundles. She discovered that the only ones that produced long, strong threads were found on mulberry trees.

Days of searching for more mulberry trees passed. Hours of gathering cocoons went by. Then the soaking, unwinding, and winding began again. Finally, Hsi-ling had enough glossy strands. With these she and her ladies wove a splendid piece of fabric, then carefully stitched the royal gift. Hsi-ling worked secretly so the emperor would not know about the surprise.

Using more strands, dyed from leaves, bark, and the rainbow-colored flowers that bobbed and bowed in the garden, Hsi-ling embroidered birds, animals, fancy designs, and the emperor's favorite scenes of China. She used much red, because red represented happiness, prosperity, and good luck. Finally, her surprise was ready.

Bowing and blushing, Hsi-ling presented her special gift, a royal robe, to her husband. She stepped back and wondered: Would Huang Ti like her gift? He already had many robes. Would it please him? She watched as he ran his fingers over the soft, shimmering fabric, smooth as a rose petal and airy as a spring breeze.

28

When his servants draped the silky robe around him, a smile spread over Huang Ti's face, and he spoke. "I am overcome with the beauty and softness of this magnificent garment. It could not have been more splendid had it been made of moonbeams and stardust. It feels as smooth as the feathers on a swan."

Then he asked Hsi-ling about it. She whispered in his ear, telling him about the tiny, mysterious spinners that created the precious bundles on the mulberry branches. She pointed to her ladies, who had secretly spun the threads for the magnificent fabric.

When Hsi-ling finished, Huang Ti raised his arms and proclaimed, "From this day forth, groves of mulberry trees will be planted. Each spring after the jade green leaves appear on the mulberry trees, the cocoons will be gathered. All the ladies of the palace will spin. The silk will be woven into magnificent robes for the royal family and into colorful banners to honor the gods."

From that time on, banners of blue silk hung in the Temple of Heaven. Yellow silk banners decorated the Temple of the Earth. Red silk banners filled the walls in the Temple of the Sun. And white silk adorned the Temple of the Moon.

Talented fingers embroidered hundreds of birds, pine trees, and peacocks on silk wall hangings. Artists painted village scenes on panels of fine silk, and poets wrote sonnets on long silk scrolls.

And all of this happened because one day, a curious young woman sat under the wide-spreading branches of a mulberry tree and dropped a silken bundle into a cup of tea.

Author's Note

Much later, Hsi-ling was declared the Goddess of Silk. For centuries, on one day each year, the empress of China would dress in the finest silk and enter the temple bearing gifts to honor Hsi-ling. Even though the legend credits Hsi-ling with the discovery, it is not known exactly who discovered silk since it dates back to before the invention of writing in China.

Silk was so important to the Chinese that taxes were often paid with silk thread or fabrics made of silk. Government salaries were paid in bolts of silk. No one could send or carry silkworms or cocoons out of China. The Roman Emperor Tiberius (AD 14–37) tried to forbid his people from wearing silk for fear that all the gold would be drained from his empire into China. For 2,000 years, the whole world depended on China to produce silk, for during that time, China alone held the secret to making the luxurious fabric.

The Life Cycle
of the
Silkworm Moth

From early times people have valued the fine silk spun by silkworms. Various legends of how silk was discovered began over 4,000 years ago, but silk was actually discovered and used much earlier. Today, embroidered pieces of silk that are about 4,500 years old are on display in the Summer Palace Museum in Hangzhou, China.

Silkworms are a stage in the life cycle of the silkworm moth; its species name is *Bombyx mori*. Moths are insects. Several million species, or types, of insects exist in the world. Most insects, including the silkworm moth, have two pairs of wings. All insects have six legs and three main body parts: a head, a thorax, and an abdomen.

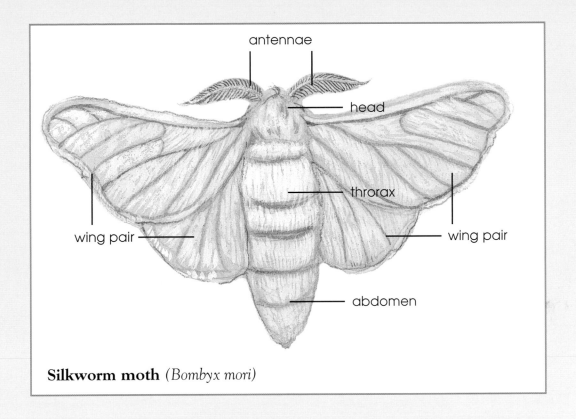

antennae

head

throrax

wing pair

wing pair

abdomen

Silkworm moth (*Bombyx mori*)

Silkworm moths also have two long feathery sense organs, called antennae, on their heads. Antennae provide the silkworm moth with the ability to smell and touch. Attached to the moth's thorax are two pairs of wings, each about 2 inches (5 cm) long. These wings are covered with tiny white scales, the "dust" that comes off on your hand when you hold a moth or butterfly.

Some insects, such as moths, butterflies, bees, and ants, go through four very different stages as they change in form from an egg to an adult. The stages in this complete metamorphosis are: egg, larva, pupa, and adult. Other insects, such as grasshoppers, crickets, and cockroaches, go through a three-stage development: egg, nymph, and adult. This is an incomplete metamorphosis.

The first stage in the silkworm moth's metamorphosis occurs after a male and a female mate. Soon after the male moth mates, he dies. The female lives a few days or weeks, long enough to lay her eggs. In her short lifetime she lays about 500 eggs, each one no larger than the head of a pin.

The female lays her pale yellow eggs on the leaves of a mulberry tree, the silkworm's special food. The moth produces a gluelike substance called sericin. It covers every egg and makes them stick to anything they touch, especially the mulberry leaves.

The second stage in the metamorphosis process is the larval stage. In three to ten days larvae, tiny wormlike creatures, hatch after biting holes in the eggs with their powerful jaws. A young silkworm is only about $1/8$-inch (3 mm) long—smaller than a grain of rice.

Silkworm moth laying eggs

Newly hatched silkworm caterpillars eating mulberry leaves

The larvae are called silkworms, but they're not actually worms. They are caterpillars with large heads and twelve simple eyes. Long black hairs cover the newly hatched silkworms and protect them from being hurt or smothered when they crowd against each other. Some hatchlings, such as ducklings or robins, look similar to their parents. However, the tiny, thin, black silkworms don't look at all like their parents—furry adult moths with white wings and thick, feathery antennae.

Silkworms spend most of their lives eating. They thrive only on the leaves from mulberry trees. Their strong jaws work like scissors when they chew. The more a silkworm eats, the bigger it grows. But its skin doesn't grow along with it. Soon the silkworm becomes too large for its skin, and it starts to molt. Molting is the process of growing a new skin and shedding the old one.

Each time the silkworm is ready to molt, it stops eating and raises its head in the air. During this time of inactivity, a new skin is forming under the old one. The silkworm produces a special liquid that dissolves layers of the old skin so that the skin gradually becomes thinner. Then the silkworm tightens its muscles and takes in a lot of air. This increases the pressure on the old skin, causing it to split. With its clawed legs, the silkworm holds onto the mulberry leaves and wiggles out of the old skin.

At first the new skin is loose and wrinkled. But as the silkworm begins eating again, the new skin becomes smooth and tight. Often a silkworm will eat its old skin. The silkworm molts four times in the larval stage. When a silkworm is about four weeks old, it stops eating and shakes its head from side to side. It's ready to spin its cocoon. This is the stage when the silkworm produces the fine silk that people use. However, that's not the reason a silkworm spins a cocoon. A cocoon's main purpose is to provide a safe, protective covering for the caterpillar during the stage when it is unable to move or defend itself.

The silkworm produces liquid silk in its silk glands. The liquid flows through a tube called the spinneret that is located near its lower lip. When the liquid silk hits the air, it becomes a solid thread. First the silkworm spins some white threads nearby to anchor its cocoon. Then it starts to spin silk around and around itself, moving its head in a figure-eight pattern. It makes the outer layer of the cocoon first, and then adds other layers from the inside.

Like the silkworm moths, silkworms also produce sericin. In the first stage of the life cycle, this gummy coating makes the moth's eggs stick to the mulberry leaves. During the larval stage, it makes the threads on the silkworm's cocoon stick together. Some silkworms complete their cocoons in two or three days of steady work. Others take a week. Many insects spin silk cocoons, but their silk is not as long or as strong at the silkworm's threads, so it's not as desirable for human use. Each silkworm cocoon is made from a single, strong, shiny, silk thread, some almost a mile long.

Silkworm caterpillar spinning a cocoon

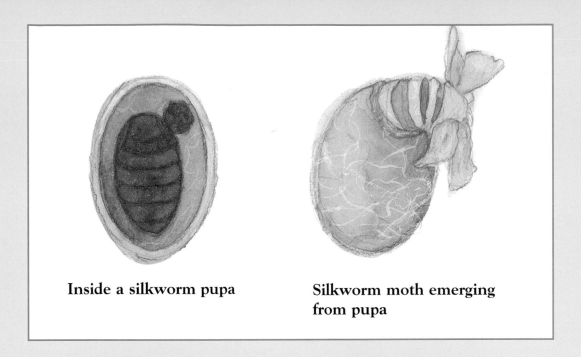

Inside a silkworm pupa   **Silkworm moth emerging from pupa**

The third stage of a silkworm's growth occurs inside the cocoon, where the silkworm is called a pupa. During the pupal stage, the silkworm molts a fifth time. After this molting it's almost 3 inches (7.6 cm) long, about the size of an adult's finger, and it weighs about 10,000 times more than when it first hatched from its egg. If an 8-pound (3.6 kg) baby grew at this rate, it would weigh 80,000 pounds (36,287 kg) by the time it was an adult!

Amazing changes take place inside the cocoon. The outer skin of the silkworm turns into a hard brown covering. Inside this rigid pupal shell the pupa rarely moves. Yet the silkworm's body transforms from that of a caterpillar into that of an adult moth. The caterpillar's short legs change into long, jointed legs. The thin wormlike body becomes a short, thick body covered with white scales. A pair of long, feathery antennae replaces the tiny sense organs on the silkworm's head. Large compound eyes and scaly wings develop.

After two to three weeks the changes are complete. The hard pupal shell splits open, and the adult moth must work to push itself out of the thick silk cocoon. To help itself emerge, the silkworm moth spits out a strong liquid that makes a hole in the cocoon. Once out of the cocoon, the silkworm moth pumps blood into the veins of its soft, crumpled, wet wings to expand and harden them. It waves its wings to dry them and then looks for a mate. Very soon the cycle starts again.

The adult female moth lays eggs

that hatch into wormlike larvae

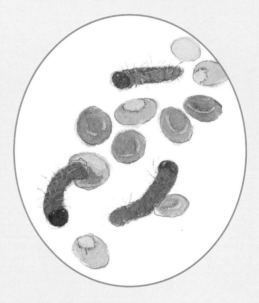

that spin cocoons in which pupae change into adult moths.

It soon breaks out of the cocoon and finds a mate. If it's a female, it will lay eggs
. . . and the stages of the life cycle starts over again.

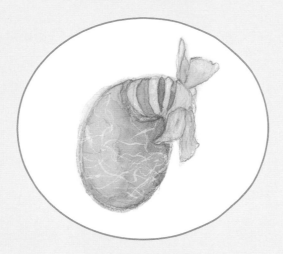

For hundreds of years people have raised and cared for silkworm moths to ensure
a better quality of silk. As a result, today's silkworm moths are more dependent
on people and less able to care for themselves than when they were wild. Today
very few silkworm moths are found in the wild. However, as long as people
desire silk, there will be a bond between man, mulberry trees, and moths. And
the silkworm moth will survive.

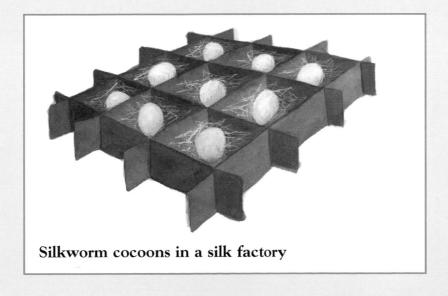

Silkworm cocoons in a silk factory

Glossary

abdomen   end part of a silkworm's body

antennae   sense organs or feelers on a silkworm moth's head

cocoon   a silky envelope spun by a silkworm to protect it during its pupal stage

compound eyes   eyes made up of many parts that can see both images and colors

emerge   come out

larva   the second stage in the development of a silkworm moth, when it is wormlike after hatching from its egg

legend   story handed down through the years that is connected with some real events but probably not true in itself

metamorphosis   the process of growing and changing that produces most adult insects

molting   the process of growing a new skin and shedding the old one

pupa   the third stage in a complete metamorphosis, when the silkworm moth is formed in the cocoon

sericin   gluelike substance that makes the threads of the cocoon stick together

silk glands   glands in the silkworm's body that produce silk

spinneret   tube on the silkworm's head through which silk is expelled

thorax   middle part of a silkworm moth's body